Playing Baseball

A Coloring Book

Copyright

All Rights reserved. No part of this book may be reproduced or used in any way or form

or by any means whether electronic or mechanical, this means that you cannot record

or photocopy any material ideas or tips that are provided in this book.

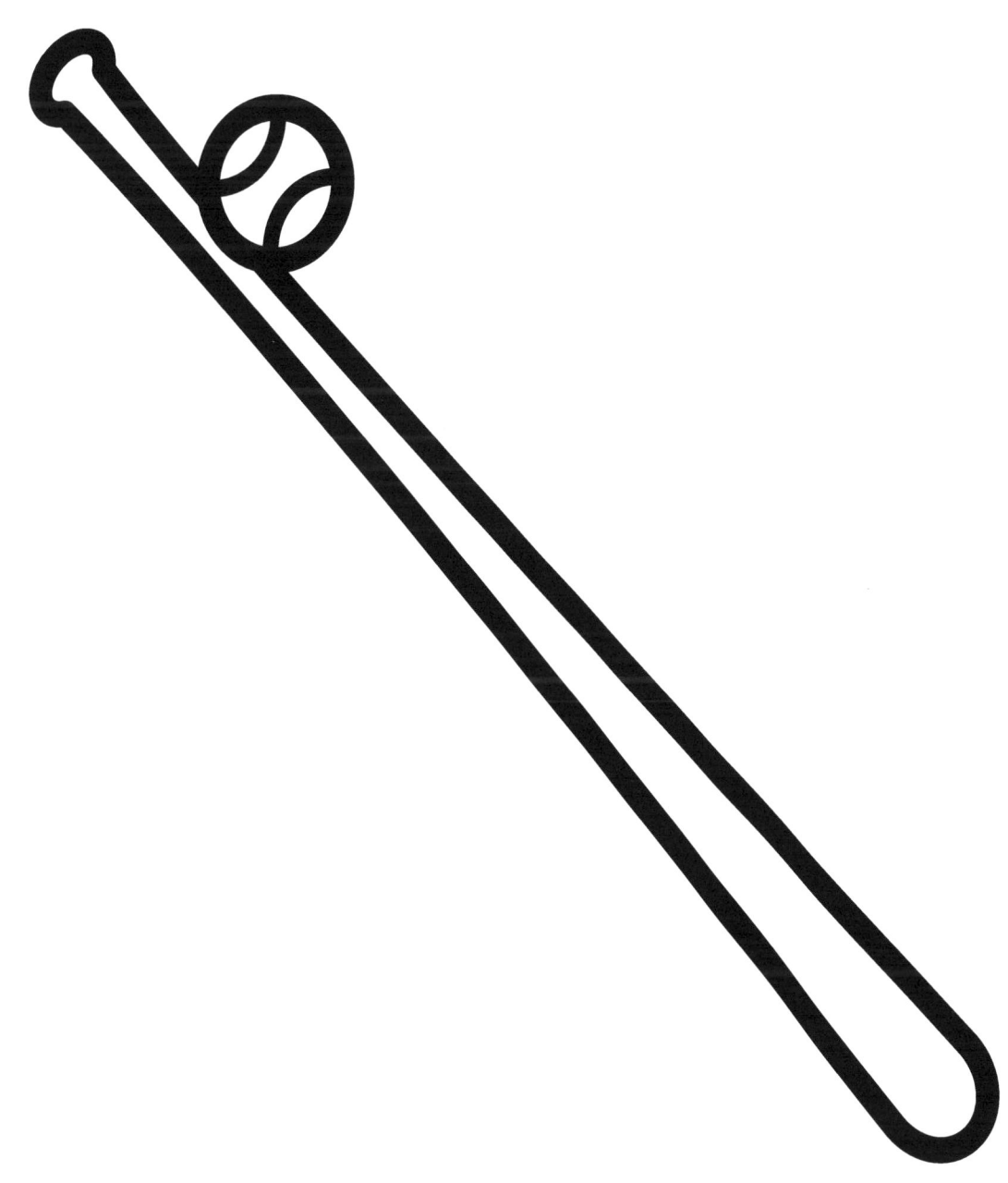

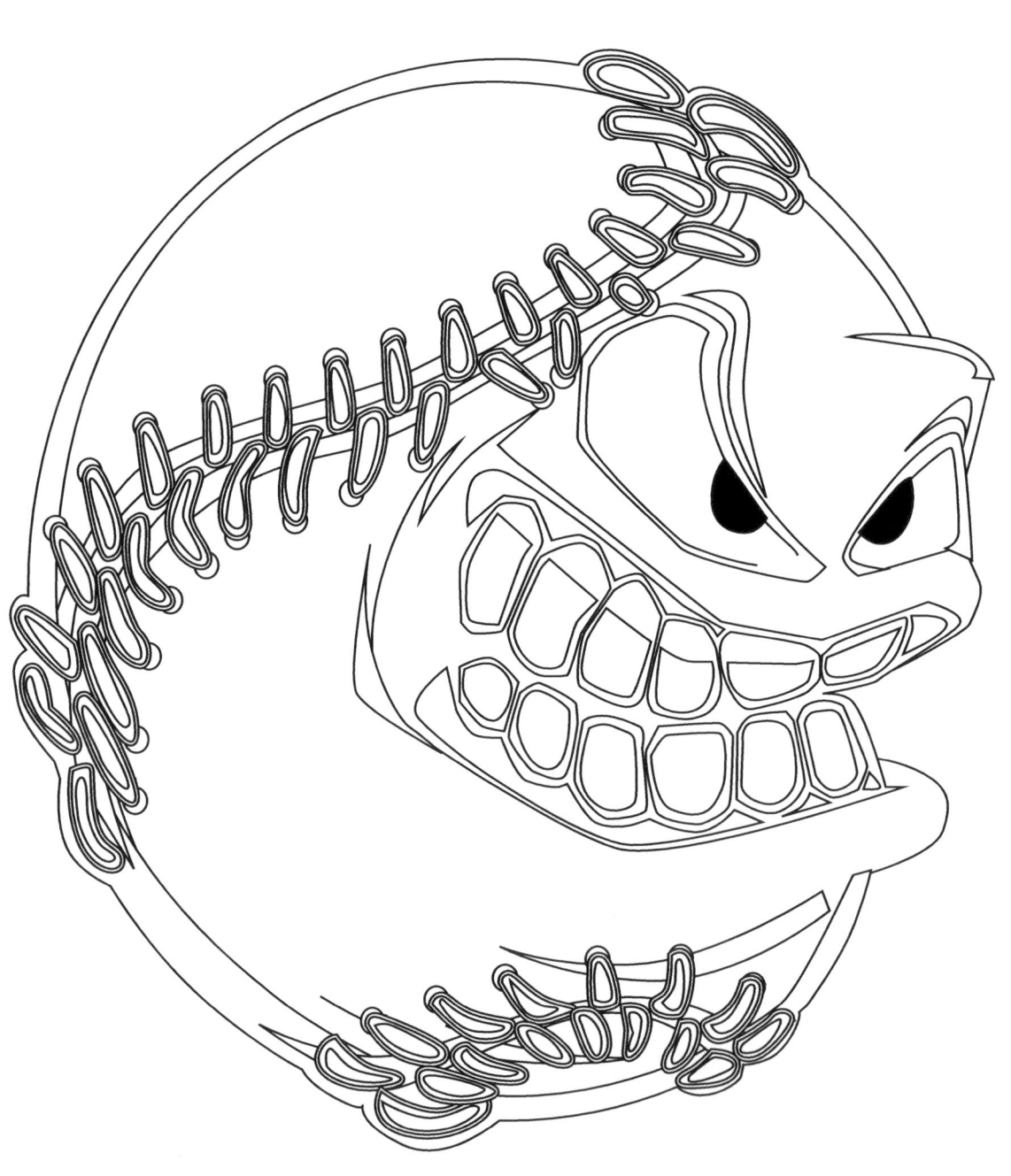

Made in the USA
San Bernardino, CA
10 August 2016